# YOUR PATRIARCHAL BLESSING

ED J. PINEGAR
RICHARD J. ALLEN

Covenant Communications, Inc.

Cover image by Mitch Hrdlicka © Photodisc Green Collection/Getty Images.

Cover design copyrighted 2005 by Covenant Communications, Inc.

Published by Covenant Communications, Inc.
American Fork, Utah

Printed in United States
First Printing: May 2005

21 20 19 18 17 16 15      14 13 12 11 10 9 8

ISBN 978-1-62108-790-8

# Your Patriarchal Blessing—A Personal Revelation

*The same Lord who provided a Liahona to Lehi provides*

*for you and for me today a rare and valuable gift to*

*give direction to our lives, to mark the hazards*

*to our safety, and to chart the way . . .*

*to our heavenly home.*

THOMAS S. MONSON

# THE JOURNEY OF LIFE

Life is a journey back home to our Father in Heaven. In His loving kindness, He has given us many blessings to help us stay on course—our family, the gospel, the scriptures, living prophets, the priesthood, the Church, and the inspiration of the Spirit. All of these things assist us in our journey day by day.

In addition, the Lord has provided a powerful tool to help us travel safely along the straight and narrow path that leads back into His presence. This tool is called a patriarchal blessing. What is a patriarchal blessing? Let's consider an analogy. When you take a journey, it's a good idea to bring a compass—a guidance system that keeps you pointed in the right direction. Your patriarchal blessing is like a personal compass because it helps you know where you are going. This personal compass operates on faith much like the Liahona that the Lord provided for Lehi and his family in the desert (see 1 Ne. 16:10, 16, 26–29).

Your patriarchal blessing is a personal treasure of wisdom to enrich and edify your life. It is a precious gift from your Father in Heaven—along with the holy scriptures and all other gospel blessings—to help you

return safely and securely back home, having traveled
faithfully and courageously.

## ONE OF GOD'S GREATEST GIFTS

Your patriarchal blessing is personal revelation to
you from Heavenly Father through one of His chosen
servants, a man who has been called and ordained for
this special purpose. Your patriarchal blessing is a statement of how your Father in Heaven looks upon you—
as one of His choice sons or daughters to whom He has
granted special gifts and talents that can help you be
happy and serve others with charity and love. Your
patriarchal blessing is the Lord's sacred way of letting
you know that you belong to His fold. We all yearn to
belong—to our family, to our circle of friends, and to
the church and kingdom of God. Belonging brings
comfort and joy, and it offers wonderful opportunities
to grow and serve others.

In your patriarchal blessing, the patriarch will be
inspired to declare your lineage through which you will
receive glorious blessings based on your faithfulness.
This lineage makes clear how you fit into God's plan for
organizing His children for the purpose of blessing the
lives of everyone in the world. You are a chosen servant
who is to play an important role of leadership in building the kingdom of God. Your patriarchal blessing
helps you to see yourself in this light by declaring to
which tribe of Israel you belong. It is a gift to you,
through one of His chosen priesthood leaders, giving

you an inspired view of who you are and who you can become by seeking and applying the gifts and blessings of God.

# KNOWING THE WILL OF YOUR FATHER IN HEAVEN

Heavenly Father loves you. You are important to Him and to His Son. Their work and glory includes bringing to pass your immortality and eternal life (see Moses 1:39). Heavenly Father and His Son want you to enjoy happiness here and in the hereafter. The Prophet Joseph Smith said, "Happiness is the object and the design of our existence" (*Teachings of the Prophet Joseph Smith*, 1976, 255). Happiness comes from living the gospel of Jesus Christ. It does not come from momentary pleasures or becoming entangled in worldly things that vanish tomorrow. Happiness comes from following in the footsteps of the Savior— doing what He would want you to do. Your patriarchal blessing helps you to stay focused on that which will bring more happiness and joy into your life. It is evidence of a loving Father in Heaven speaking to you *by name* and giving you assurance that He will help you find the way to happiness.

Heavenly Father has established a pattern to reveal His will and blessings to His children here upon the earth. It is called revelation. When He speaks to the Church as a whole, He speaks through His prophet. But He also speaks to individuals through personal revelation to help them succeed in their own callings and circles of activity. This revelation comes through the inspiration of the Holy Ghost to those who are faithful and humble, praying for divine counsel and guidance. Everyone is entitled to receive revelation from Heavenly Father because He is no respecter of persons. No matter what your situation might be now or in the future—young or old, son or daughter, husband or wife, father or mother—Heavenly Father wants to bless you and guide you. He is the Father of all mankind, and He seeks to bless all of His children.

Personal revelation also comes to individuals through the avenue of a patriarchal blessing. All who seek to know the will of Heavenly Father with real intent, having faith, can receive revelation from Heavenly Father through His Spirit. He has set up a system within His kingdom and church here upon the earth whereby you can receive a special priesthood blessing—a patriarchal blessing—under the inspiration of your stake patriarch as he is directed by the Spirit. This is like having your very own section of the Doctrine and Covenants—a revelation especially for you.

President Spencer W. Kimball taught the following:

> The patriarch is a prophet entitled to the revelations of the Lord to each individual on whose head he places his hands. He may indicate the lineage of the individual, but he may also pour out blessings that are prophetic to the individual for his life. We hope the people of this land will avail themselves of this great blessing.

The blessings which he gives are conditional. They are promised, as are most other blessings that the Lord has promised to people, contingent upon their worthiness and fulfilling the obligations. There is no guarantee that the blessings will be fulfilled unless the individual subscribes to the program, but I bear my testimony to you that none of the blessings he pronounces will fail if the participant of the blessing fully subscribes. (*The Teachings of Spencer W. Kimball,* 1982, 504)

This personal revelation—this patriarchal blessing—can become a Liahona for your life, much like the Lord provided the brass ball or compass of faith for Lehi and his family as they traveled through the wilderness. Here is the account of that remarkable compass from the Book of Mormon:

And it came to pass that as my father arose in the morning, and went forth to the tent door, to his great astonishment he beheld upon the ground a round ball of curious workmanship; and it was of fine brass. And within the ball were two spindles; and the one pointed the way whither we should go into the wilderness. . . .

And we did go forth again in the wilderness, following the same direction, keeping in the most fertile parts of the wilderness, . . .

And it came to pass that I, Nephi, beheld the pointers which were in the ball, that they did work according to the faith and diligence and heed which we did give unto them.

And there was also written upon them a new writing, which was plain to be read, which did give us understanding concerning the ways of the Lord; and it was written and changed from time to time, according to the faith and diligence which we gave unto it. And thus we see that by small means the Lord can bring about great things. (1 Ne. 16:10, 14, 28–29; compare Alma 37:38–45)

A patriarchal blessing, though not typically of great length, can have enormous impact on your life. The words of this blessing can shed a brilliant light across the landscape of your mortal experience and help you find your way in righteousness and faith to the presence of your Father in Heaven and His Beloved Son. We can apply the words of Nephi to our own lives in regard to a patriarchal blessing: "And thus we see that by small means the Lord can bring about great things" (1 Ne. 16:29).

Thomas S. Monson has confirmed this principle:

The same Lord who provided a Liahona to Lehi provides for you and for me today a rare and valuable gift to give direction to our lives, to mark the hazards to our safety, and to chart the way, even safe passage—not to a promised land, but to our heavenly home. The gift to which I refer is known as your patriarchal blessing. Every worthy member of the Church is entitled to receive such a precious and priceless personal treasure. ("Your Patriarchal Blessing: A Liahona of Light," *Ensign*, Nov. 1986, 65)

The Liahona directed Lehi's colony to the promised land. Similarly, your patriarchal blessing can give you direction in your life. As with all gifts and blessings from God, the fulfillment of this blessing is predicated upon your faith, your diligence, and your obedience to what the Lord says to you through the patriarch. When Lehi's family gave heed to the Liahona in faith, they were directed in their journey. In the same way, when you give heed to your patriarchal blessing, it can become a compass for your life to guide you back to the presence of our Heavenly Father.

Life includes many trials and tribulations. You can and will be called upon to solve problems and rise above adversity. There will be some significant challenges to overcome. Your patriarchal blessing can give you comfort, confirming that things will be all right if you will follow the direction of our Heavenly Father. Sister Virginia Pearce once said, "Heavenly Father and Jesus Christ live and they are in charge of this world. They know me. They love me. They have a plan for my future. I will obey the commandments, work hard, and trust in their plan. Sooner or later, everything will be okay" ("Faith Is the Answer," *Ensign,* May 1994, 92).

You can face the rest of life with courage, knowing that you can have personal direction from your Father in Heaven. We are all placed here to be tested. The

Lord said: "We will prove them herewith, to see if they will do all things whatsoever the Lord their God shall command them" (Abr. 3:25). Think of what you have to assist you. You have the scriptures, the guidance of the Holy Spirit, the counsel of our living prophets and other leaders, your priesthood blessings, and your personal prayers—all of which can give you inspired direction. In addition, you have your priceless patriarchal blessing, a most special and sacred personal revelation. Heavenly Father does not leave you alone. He has provided all of these things to help you in your sojourn here upon the earth. We can all be grateful for the mercy and kindness of Heavenly Father in providing such a unique and spiritual gift to His children.

## THE PURPOSE OF YOUR PATRIARCHAL BLESSING

In a letter to all stake presidents dated June 28, 1957, the First Presidency (David O. McKay, Stephen L. Richards, and J. Reuben Clark Jr.) gave the following definition and explanation:

> Patriarchal blessings contemplate an inspired declaration of the lineage of the recipient, and also where so moved upon by the Spirit, an inspired and prophetic statement of the life mission of the recipient, together with such blessings, cautions, and admonitions as the patriarch may be prompted to give for the accomplishment

of such life's mission, it being always made clear that the realization of all promised blessings is conditioned upon faithfulness to the gospel of our Lord, whose servant the patriarch is. All such blessings are recorded and generally only one such blessing should be adequate for each person's life. The sacred nature of the patriarchal blessing must of necessity urge all patriarchs to most earnest solicitation of divine guidance for their prophetic utterances and superior wisdom for cautions and admonitions. (Bruce R. McConkie, *Mormon Doctrine*, 1966, 558)

Patriarchs declare lineage in patriarchal blessings. Most members of the Church are the seed of Abraham through the lineage of Joseph, one of the sons of Jacob, or Israel, as he was called (see the Lineage of Israel chart on pages 12–13). As the gospel spreads throughout the earth, the fold of the Good Shepherd is enlarged through the influx of righteous and faithful Saints from all lands and cultures. Thus the kingdom of God grows by gathering in the scattered remnants of Israel from the four quarters of the earth and by adopting into the fold many sons and daughters of God of different origins and backgrounds. All are alike before God. All become the seed of Abraham through the unifying gospel of Jesus Christ. As the seed of Abraham, we have a great responsibility regarding the salvation of mankind here upon the earth, for our commission is to carry the gospel message to the entire world. Our patriarchal blessing is a vital blessing to us

*LISTS OF THE TWELVE TRIBES usually exclude Levi and Joseph. This is because, as the tribe of priests, the Levites do not inherit any land. Also, because Joseph received the birthright, he is entitled to a double portion of inheritance relative to his siblings, giving him rights to two portions (given to his sons, Mannaseh and Ephraim) in the promised land.*

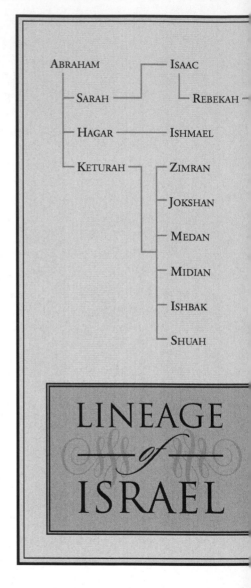

ABRAHAM — ISAAC

SARAH — REBEKAH

HAGAR — ISHMAEL

KETURAH — ZIMRAN

JOKSHAN

MEDAN

MIDIAN

ISHBAK

SHUAH

# LINEAGE
## *of*
# ISRAEL

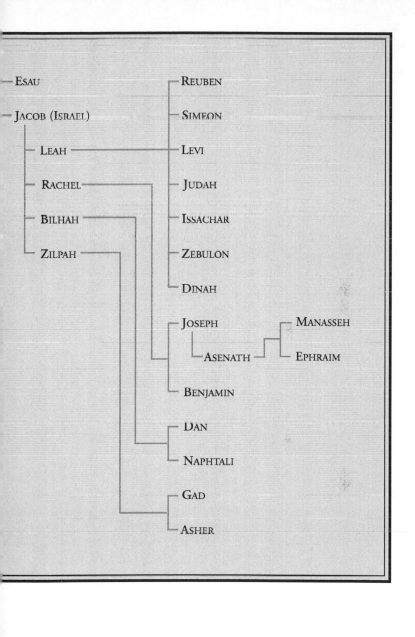

Esau

Jacob (Israel)

Leah

Rachel

Bilhah

Zilpah

Reuben

Simeon

Levi

Judah

Issachar

Zebulon

Dinah

Joseph

Asenath

Benjamin

Dan

Naphtali

Gad

Asher

Manasseh

Ephraim

because it confirms that we belong to God's family and declares a specific lineage through which our blessings can flow.

It is the office and calling of a patriarch in giving a patriarchal blessing to identify, by the Spirit of revelation, the lineage of those whom he blesses. President Joseph Fielding Smith taught:

> The patriarch has the right by revelation to declare the lineage of those who are blessed. It is true that we are of mixed lineage. A man said to be of the lineage of Ephraim may also be a "descendant of Reuben, Benjamin or Simeon," but the blood that predominates is the one that counts. Therefore, two brothers could be assigned to a different lineage. I call your attention to the difference between Jacob and Esau. (*Answers to Gospel Questions,* 1957–66, 5:167)

President Joseph Fielding Smith shed further light on this subject of lineage as follows:

> A patriarch giving a blessing has the right of inspiration to declare the literal descent of the person receiving the blessing; he does not have authority to assign that individual to any tribe. Through the waters of baptism and the priesthood, Church members become heirs of Abraham with all the rights belonging to the children of Abraham through their faithfulness. (*Doctrines of Salvation,* 3:171)

Along with the rights belonging to the children of Abraham, members of the Church also become heirs to the responsibilities of the children of Abraham.

> The promises given to Abraham are not figurative. He was expressly told they were to extend to his "literal seed, or the seed of the body" (Abraham 2:11). If those of the Bible-believing world properly understood the promises given to Abraham, they would know that the blessings of the priesthood are essential to salvation and that the right to hold the priesthood was given to Abraham and his posterity. It is his seed that are to bear the message of the gospel to all the ends of the earth. Missionaries are expected to have received their patriarchal blessing before they begin their missions. Thus they will have a revealed confirmation that they are of the lineage that has a rightful claim to the priesthood and the attendant responsibility to declare the message of salvation to the ends of the earth. (Joseph Fielding McConkie, *Answers: Straightforward Answers to Tough Gospel Questions,* 1998, 184)

The counsels, reprimands, and blessings given by Jacob to the twelve tribes of Israel are recorded in Genesis 49. We must remember that the House of Israel is the Lord's chosen designation for His people, and all who come unto Christ come within the blessings of Abraham and the House of Israel as Elder Bruce R. McConkie describes:

Jacob's name was changed to *Israel*, "for as a prince," the divine decree announced, "hast thou power with God and with men, and hast prevailed." (Gen. 32:24–30; 35:9–13; Hos. 12:1–5.) Literally, the name Israel means *contender with God*, the sense and meaning indicating one who has succeeded in his supplication before the Lord, who has enlisted as a *soldier of God*, who has become a *prince of God*.

By divine command the name was applied to the 12 tribes collectively. (Gen. 49:28; Ex. 3:16.) Hundreds of millions of persons have thus been Israelites, heirs of the promises made to their fathers. (*Mormon Doctrine*, 1966, 389; italics in original)

In the end, the tribes will come together as the house of Israel. Elder McConkie states:

"And they shall be filled with songs of everlasting joy. Behold, this is the blessing of the everlasting God upon the tribes of Israel, and the richer blessing upon the head of Ephraim and his fellows. And they also of the tribe of Judah, after their pain shall be sanctified in holiness before the Lord, to dwell in his presence day and night, forever and ever." (D&C 133:25–35; Isa. 35:1–10.) Thus the ancient kingdom of Ephraim with its Ten Tribes and the kingdom of Judah with the smaller portion of Israel shall once again become "one nation in the land upon the mountains of Israel; . . . and they shall be no more two nations, neither shall they be divided into two kingdoms any more at all: . . . so shall they be my people, and I will be their God." (Ezek. 37:22–23.) (Bruce R. McConkie, *The Millennial Messiah: The Second Coming of the Son of Man,* 1982, 329)

Besides a declaration of your lineage, your patriarchal blessing identifies for you certain blessings and gifts. You may be admonished to do certain things and be given advice for your life's journey. You may also be cautioned or made aware of certain things that might be concerns for you. These blessings, admonitions, and cautions are important—and each of them will play an important part as you read and reread your blessing.

Your patriarchal blessing extends in scope to your entire life, even from the beginning to the end. Remember that blessings might apply not only to the present earth life, but that they often apply to the life hereafter as well. Not all blessings are fulfilled entirely upon the earth but are often realized in times to come.

## SOME EXAMPLES

To learn how this wonderful process can affect our lives, let us look at some excerpts from patriarchal blessings given by the Prophet Joseph Smith's father, the first patriarch to the Church in this latter-day dispensation, who served in that capacity from December 18, 1833, until his death in 1840 (see *History of the Church,* 4:189–91). We are not comparing these blessings to what your own blessing might say, but rather illustrating how a patriarchal blessing can and should be a source of direction for your life.

Patriarchal blessings give directions, charting the course for the faithful as they traverse the waters of life. In the blessing given to Martha Jane Knowlton Coray, for example, she was promised that nothing could overthrow her if she was faithful, that she would have power to overcome life's difficulties, that she should not marry outside of the Church, "for this is contrary to the order of heaven," and that if she was faithful the Lord would "guide her through the slippery paths of youth" and direct her in finding a proper marriage partner, who would join with her in raising children. The knowledge of these promises became a guide and director for her throughout her life.

Emeline Grover Rich relates that in her blessing, Father Smith promised that someday she would become a nurse and bring relief to many people. She had had the desire to become a nurse, she records, from age nine, but no doubt the effect of the patriarchal blessing was to encourage her to further prepare herself and sharpen her focus. She observed that, years after receiving the blessing, while living in Paris, Idaho, she "was called upon a great deal to go out among the sick, there being no doctors or drug stores, and," she wrote, "I had very good success; after a little I was called up to tend the sick both temporally and spiritually and I was set apart [by Brigham Young] for that work."

In the instance of Edward Stevenson, his patriarchal blessing became a standard against which he measured his progress and worthiness in the kingdom. He recorded that Father Smith had said (using a biblical metaphor) that he was one who was appointed to push the Saints together. He wrote that in 1847, thirteen years after receiving his blessing, he was "a captain of ten under Charles C. Rich, thereby helping to push the people together; and in 1855, I had a charge of a company of Saints from Liverpool to Philadelphia, thence to St. Louis and on to the frontier [of] Atchison, Kansas, called by our people 'Mormon Grove'; and from there to Zion, in charge of the 'Texas Company.'" He concludes this recitation of some of what he considered major events in his life by saying, "I only mention this here in connection with my patriarchal blessing, and the words of Moses in Deut. 33:17," which Father Smith had used in his blessing. For Stevenson, knowing that he was doing things that fulfilled patriarchal promises left him with the assurance that the Lord approved of the course he was pursuing in life. (Mark L. McConkie, *The Father of the Prophet: Stories and Insights from the Life of Joseph Smith, Sr.,* 1993, 94–95)

Looking back at these inspirational blessings, we are reminded of the long tradition of patriarchal blessings throughout the history of God's dealings with His people. When Joseph Smith Sr. was installed as patriarch to the Church, his son, the Prophet Joseph Smith, pronounced the following words that recall the pattern set by the ancient patriarch Adam in blessing his children:

Blessed of the Lord is my father, for he shall stand in the midst of his posterity and shall be comforted by their blessings when he is old and bowed down with years, and shall be called a prince over them, and shall be numbered among those who hold the right of Patriarchal Priesthood, even the keys of that ministry: for he shall assemble together his posterity like unto Adam; and the assembly which he called shall be an example for my father, for thus it is written of him:

Three years previous to the death of Adam, he called Seth, Enos, Cainan, Mahalaleel, Jared, Enoch and Methuselah, who were High Priests, with the residue of his posterity, who were right-eous, into the valley of Adam-ondi-Ahman, and there bestowed upon them his last blessing. And the Lord appeared unto them, and they rose up and blessed Adam, and called him Michael, the Prince, the Archangel. And the Lord adminis-tered comfort unto Adam, and said unto him, I have set thee to be at the head: a multitude of nations shall come of thee, and thou art a Prince over them forever.

So shall it be with my father: he shall be called a prince over his posterity, holding the keys of the patriarchal Priesthood over the kingdom of God on earth, even the Church of the Latter-day Saints, and he shall sit in the general assembly of Patriarchs, even in council with the Ancient of Days when he shall sit and all the Patriarchs with him and shall enjoy his right and authority under the direction of the Ancient of Days. (*Teachings of the Prophet Joseph Smith*, 1976, 38)

This pattern of bestowing patriarchal blessings was carried on in succeeding dispensations. Abraham, Isaac, Jacob, Lehi, Alma, and other great men bestowed upon their sons and daughters magnificent blessings and counsel under the inspiration of the Almighty. You too, as a partaker of this holy heritage, have the opportunity to receive a blessing under the hands of an ordained patriarch, as well as blessings from your father and other priesthood leaders.

President Gordon B. Hinckley gained valuable insight from his patriarchal blessing as he was traveling to his mission as a young elder:

While on board ship, Elder Hinckley pulled out the patriarchal blessing he had received at age eleven from patriarch Thomas E. Callister. He couldn't remember having read it since the day the patriarch had come to the Hinckley home and pronounced blessings upon him and several of his brothers and sisters, but now he was interested in reviewing those promises made a dozen years earlier. "Thou shalt grow to the full stature of manhood and shall become a mighty and valiant leader in the midst of Israel," the patriarch had promised. "The Holy Priesthood shall be thine to enjoy and thou shalt minister in the midst of Israel as only those can who are called of God. Thou shalt ever be a messenger of peace; the nations of the earth shall hear thy voice and be brought to a knowledge of the truth by the wonderful testimony which thou shalt bear." Perhaps, he thought, this mission to England would fulfill at least one part of his blessing—that he would bear testimony to the *nations* (England and the United States being a plurality) of the earth. (Sheri L. Dew, *Go Forward with Faith: The Biography of Gordon B. Hinckley,* 1996, 60, emphasis in original)

## THE PATRIARCH AND HOW BLESSINGS ARE GIVEN

The Church provides at least one patriarch in each stake. He is a worthy and spiritually mature high priest who is called and ordained for the blessing of the Saints. The Doctrine and Covenants states, "It is the duty of the Twelve, in all large branches of the church, to ordain evangelical ministers, as they shall be designated unto them by revelation" (D&C 107:39). The term *evangelical ministers* or *evangelists* (as in the sixth Article of Faith) is understood to mean "patriarchs." The Prophet Joseph

Smith taught: "An Evangelist is a Patriarch. . . . Wherever the Church of Christ is established in the earth, there should be a Patriarch for the benefit of the posterity of the Saints, as it was with Jacob in giving his patriarchal blessing unto his sons" (*HC* 3:381).

The responsibility to call patriarchs is now generally delegated by the Quorum of the Twelve to stake presidents. As commentator Ariel S. Ballif has pointed out, "The training and preparation of patriarchs includes spiritual enhancement through prayer and righteous living, constant study of the scriptural and historical heritage of the calling, and occasional meetings where they are instructed by their leaders" (*Encyclopedia of Mormonism*, 1992, 1065).

Aside from giving blessings to members of his stake, a stake patriarch is also permitted to give patriarchal blessings to members of his own family. Patriarchal blessings are recorded as they are given and then later transcribed in written format. The original copy is forwarded to the patriarchal division of the Church Historical Department. The individual receives a copy from the patriarch as a sacred guide for life—a personal scripture from the Lord.

# FREQUENTLY ASKED QUESTIONS

*When should I receive my patriarchal blessing?*

There is no set age for receiving a patriarchal blessing. The time might be right when you can meet the following qualifications:

- You have been a member of the Church for at least one year.

- You have a strong desire to receive your blessing.

- You are humble and easily entreated, with a willingness to receive direction from the Lord.

- You have faith that the blessing will be inspired of the Lord.

- You understand the significance of the lineage of the seed of Abraham and the responsibility placed upon those who are of this lineage.

- You have sufficient maturity to read and comprehend the gifts, blessings, admonitions, and cautions that are given to you during the blessing.

- You have the faith to accept, and an eagerness to live to fulfill, your patriarchal blessing.

All of these things will help you be prepared to receive your patriarchal blessing.

*How is a patriarchal blessing given?*
A patriarchal blessing is given by the laying on of hands by the stake patriarch and through the inspiration of the Holy Spirit. It is revelation from God through the stake patriarch to you as a child of God.

# Preparing for Your Patriarchal Blessing

*Organize yourselves; prepare every needful thing.*

—Doctrine and Covenants 88:119

# A CHECKLIST OF HOW
# TO PREPARE SPIRITUALLY

The Lord does not require perfection, but He does require that you have a willing heart and a desire to do good. The Savior gave us this standard to follow as members of His Church and kingdom:

> And ye shall offer for a sacrifice unto me a broken heart and a contrite spirit. And whoso cometh unto me with a broken heart and a contrite spirit, him will I baptize with fire and with the Holy Ghost. . . .
>
> Therefore, whoso repenteth and cometh unto me as a little child, him will I receive, for of such is the kingdom of God. Behold, for such I have laid down my life, and have taken it up again; therefore repent, and come unto me ye ends of the earth, and be saved. (3 Ne. 9:20, 22)

Within the framework of this attitude and inner conviction, you can prepare yourself for greater and greater blessings. Heavenly Father wishes to bless you, and He has reserved specific blessings for you.

Here are some things you can do to become better prepared to receive your patriarchal blessing:

*Cultivate a Desire*

It is important that you have a desire to receive your blessing, for desire is often a precursor to change. It is the motivation within that causes you to want to do good and to be good. If you desire to receive a patriarchal blessing you will be more eager to apply it to your life. Dallin H. Oaks discussed righteous desires as follows:

> The scriptures say that when we desire righteousness our "heart is right" with God. The Psalmist condemned the people of ancient Israel because "their heart was not right with [God]" (Psalms 78:37). When King Solomon blessed the people at the dedication of the temple, he concluded with these words: "Let your heart therefore be perfect with the Lord our God, to walk in his statutes, and to keep his commandments, as at this day" (1 Kings 8:61). (*Pure in Heart,* 1988, 4)

With a sincere desire in place, you will prepare your mind for the wonderful experience of receiving a patriarchal blessing.

*Show Humility*

Humility is sometimes referred to as the beginning of exaltation or the cardinal virtue of growth. When you are humble, you are willing and able to receive direction from the Lord. But more important, you have a relationship with and a dependence upon God. You realize that you are totally subject to Him. When you are in a state of humility, you will be submissive, teachable, and willing to receive His counsel. This is why humility is a key in understanding and making use of your patriarchal blessing.

You can fast and pray to show your humility and seek the Spirit. Prayer is very personal, and your Heavenly Father will speak to you if you will but ask. As you prepare for your patriarchal blessing, pray for inspiration and guidance, pray for understanding, pray for the patriarch, and pray that all who might come to your blessing be filled with the Spirit. By fasting beforehand, you will be in a mode of readiness to receive the blessings of the Lord. Prayer and fasting show the Lord that you are anxious and willing to submit to His will by offering a broken heart and a contrite spirit.

### Exercise Faith

Exercising faith brings power into your life. Faith is the first principle of the gospel of Jesus Christ. Faith is not only a belief and a hope for things that are true, but it also moves us to action and empowers our life—for faith is the power by which all things are done (see Joseph Smith, *Lectures on Faith*). As you exercise your faith, you will be in a state of readiness to receive the Lord's guidance and blessings, and you will also invite the spiritual influence of heaven into your life. Through faith, you receive the blessings of God. Through faith, you can be healed. Through faith, you can understand the things you must know. The effects of your patriarchal blessing will be enhanced as you exercise your faith in God and in Jesus Christ, in the patriarch, and in yourself—to be all that the Lord would have you be.

Doing these things will put you in a state of spiritual readiness. As the prophet Jacob mentioned, "to be carnally-minded is death, and to be spiritually-minded is life eternal" (2 Ne. 9:39). When you prepare yourself to be spiritually minded, you receive the blessings and the companionship of the Holy Spirit in your life. You become Spirit directed. You are inspired to do that which is right and good. Spirituality is the presence of the Spirit in your life. Should this not be one of the greatest goals in your life? As the Spirit is with you, you will have no desire to do evil but to do good continually. With the Spirit upon you, you can receive the blessings of the Lord—in this case a patriarchal blessing that can direct you throughout your life.

"Organize yourselves; prepare every needful thing," commanded the Lord (D&C 88:119; 109:8). As you prepare every needful thing, you will be better able to receive the blessings of Heavenly Father through your experience with the patriarch. Remember—if there is anything you need to repent of, it is important that you do so that you may become clean and pure. Your bishop can help you in this process. Worthiness is a key to receiving the blessings of the Spirit. A patriarchal blessing is a spiritual experience that opens up to you the channels of personal revelation from God. As you improve your life and do that which is right, you will stay in tune with the Spirit and thus be prepared for the words that the patriarch will speak to you under inspiration.

## A CHECKLIST OF OTHER IMPORTANT THINGS TO DO

While it is important to prepare yourself spiritually to receive your patriarchal blessing, you must also make sure that you are prepared physically to receive your blessing. Doing so will help you focus on the spiritual nature of your blessing.

- Schedule and have an interview with your bishop. He will ask you questions to discern your worthiness and will, when appropriate, issue you a recommend to receive your patriarchal blessing.

- If your blessing will be given by a patriarch outside your stake, make an appointment for your stake president to countersign your recommend.

- Contact the patriarch to arrange a time for your blessing to take place.

- Invite close family members or loved ones, in advance, to attend your blessing.

- Dress in appropriate Sunday clothes for your patriarchal blessing, and remind your family members and loved ones to do the same.

- Prepare in advance to arrive at least fifteen minutes early for your appointment with the patriarch.

## LOOKING FORWARD TO YOUR PATRIARCHAL BLESSING

Let's imagine what it might be like when you receive your patriarchal blessing. You have prayerfully prepared yourself for this experience. You have talked with your bishop and other priesthood leaders and family members about the nature and purpose of a patriarchal blessing. You have studied the word of God (relevant passages of scripture and words of the living prophets) to the best of your ability. Even though you might feel somewhat nervous and apprehensive, your mind and heart are full of faith and peace as you anticipate this blessing. It will occur but one time in your life. Now that time has come.

You are ready. You dress in your Sunday clothes and go with close family members or loved ones to visit the patriarch—either in a special room at the stake center or, more likely, at the home of the patriarch. You sense a spirit of kindness as you meet the patriarch. He welcomes you and puts you at ease. He comforts you with his words of encouragement. You have a prayer together. Then, when the moment is right, as you take your place on a designated chair, he lays his hands upon your head and speaks the words of inspiration that come from Heavenly Father through the Holy Ghost. He doesn't know ahead of time what he will say; he speaks the words that come to him from the Lord. It is as if the Lord Himself had placed His hands upon your head, speaking to you personally.

When the pronouncement of the blessing is complete, the patriarch removes his hands from your head and greets you once more with a spirit of charity. All present are touched with awe at the spiritual feast that has been granted. You feel God's love for you. As you prayerfully look to God with thanksgiving, you know that He has spoken to you through the patriarch. You have a deeper sense of your identity as a child of God. You have a deeper desire to serve Him and keep His commandments. The patriarch arranges for you to receive a written copy of the recorded blessing, and you feel motivated to read and reread the words of inspiration intended to be a guide for your life.

As you leave, you thank the patriarch for his service. You thank your family members and loved ones for their encouragement and support. You find the opportunity very soon to kneel humbly in prayer to thank your Father in Heaven for this most remarkable experience and to ask Him for His help as you prepare to follow His counsel and fulfill your patriarchal blessing day by day.

Your experience may not exactly follow this pattern, but be assured that receiving your patriarchal blessing will be one of the most memorable times in your life. Your patriarchal blessing is a major milestone in your journey toward happiness. It is your precious personal revelation. It is scripture to you—just as the Bible, the Book of Mormon, the Doctrine and Covenants, and the Pearl of Great Price are scripture to the entire Church and to all who receive them as the word of God. If ever you feel inclined to ask, "Does God love me?" you can turn to the scriptures—and to your own personal patriarchal blessing—as evidence of His love. Your faith will be strengthened and your resolve will be fortified through your patriarchal blessing, for that is the Lord's intent.

# FREQUENTLY ASKED QUESTIONS

*How can I best prepare to receive my patriarchal blessing?*

You should prepare every needful thing by being spiritually ready to receive this special blessing. Praying and fasting would be appropriate. Study the scriptures. Ponder and pray about the things of the Lord. Whatever draws you closer to God by the power of the Spirit will help you prepare. The important thing is to be spiritually ready and humble so that you can receive the blessing in faith and gratitude. Exercise your faith and prayers in behalf of the patriarch so that he can be blessed likewise in the administration of your blessing.

*What is required to receive a patriarchal blessing?*

An interview with your bishop is required. He will recommend you, based on your worthiness, to receive a patriarchal blessing from your stake patriarch. If your blessing is to be given by a stake patriarch outside of your stake, your recommend will need to be counter-signed by the stake president. This recommend vouches for your worthiness and desire to receive your patriarchal blessing.

# HOW TO READ AND UNDERSTAND YOUR PATRIARCHAL BLESSING

*None of us knows the wisdom of the Lord. We do not know in advance exactly how He would get us from where we are to where we need to be, but He does offer us broad outlines in our patriarchal blessings.*

—JAMES E. FAUST

# FOLLOW THE SPIRIT

When you receive your patriarchal blessing, you will feel that the patriarch is an honorable and faithful priesthood leader who is inspired in his calling. He will speak to you as he is moved upon by the Holy Ghost. He will say words that are not his own, but rather those that come from Heavenly Father—just for you. The Spirit teaches the truth. That is why understanding your patriarchal blessing is a spiritual process. You are to follow the Spirit when you read your blessing and ponder its meaning.

This process of understanding through the Spirit is explained in the scriptures.

> Therefore, why is it that ye cannot understand and know, that he that receiveth the word by the Spirit of truth receiveth it as it is preached by the Spirit of truth?
>
> Wherefore, he that preacheth and he that receiveth, understand one another, and both are edified and rejoice together.
>
> And that which doth not edify is not of God, and is darkness.

That which is of God is light; and he that receiveth light, and continueth in God, receiveth more light; and that light groweth brighter and brighter until the perfect day. (D&C 50:21–24)

Your patriarchal blessing is light—spiritual light—given through the Holy Ghost. You can understand the message of your blessing by listening and pondering in a spiritual way. Thus your blessing is both given and understood through the Spirit, "and by the power of the Holy Ghost ye may know the truth of all things" (Moro. 10:5).

Marion G. Romney explained as follows how to tap into this spiritual truth:

If you want to obtain and keep the guidance of the Spirit, you can do so by following this simple four-point program.

One, *pray.* Pray diligently. Pray with each other. Pray in public in the proper places. . . .

Learn to talk to the Lord; call upon his name in great faith and confidence.

Second, *study* and learn the gospel.

Third, *live righteously;* repent of your sins by confessing them and forsaking them. Then conform to the teachings of the gospel.

Fourth, *give service* in the Church. . . .

If you will do these things, you will get the guidance of the Holy Spirit and you will go through this world successfully, regardless of what the people of the world say or do.

# REMEMBER TO LISTEN CAREFULLY TO THE LORD WITH AN ATTITUDE OF OBEDIENCE

As you study the scriptures, you will read many cases where the Lord speaks to His prophets and they respond readily and with full devotion. Do you recall the time where the prophet Alma was sent to visit the people in the city of Ammonihah who had slipped from the pathway of righteousness and had lapsed into sinful ways? Alma tried everything he could to bring the people back into the fold of the Lord, but they would not listen. When he became dejected and decided to move on to another city, an angel of the Lord intercepted him and commanded him to return to the city. As the Book of Mormon reports, "he returned speedily to the land of Ammonihah" (Alma 8:18), where he continued his ministry. In other words, he did as he was commanded. There is a great lesson for all of us in this story and similar stories about the devotion of the prophets of God.

Do you remember when the Lord commanded Adam to offer the firstlings of his flock as a sacrifice and the angel came to Adam and said, "Why dost thou offer sacrifices unto the Lord?" Adam replied, "I know not, save the Lord commanded me" (Moses 5:6). In other words, he didn't fully understand all the reasons why, but Adam was faithfully obedient.

Do you remember when Nephi was told to slay Laban? He declared, "Never at any time have I shed the blood of man" (1 Ne. 4:10). He sought understanding. The angel explained to him why it was important to obtain the sacred plates and to have the records so that his family and their descendants might have the light of the gospel in their lives. He said, "It is better that one man should perish than that a nation should dwindle and perish in unbelief" (1 Ne. 4:13). And because Nephi understood, he obeyed.

Similarly, understanding and applying your patriarchal blessing to your life requires faithful, exact, courageous obedience—obedience to the word of the Lord. It is interesting to note that every time the Lord speaks through revelation to His prophets—or in your case, through your patriarchal blessing—it is to bless our lives, to help us grow so that we can return to His presence.

Now the question is, How do you apply your patriarchal blessing to your life? Remember, each time you read your blessing, you will see different things. You will perceive a different emphasis at different times in your life. What you perceive in reading your blessing when you are a teenager may be different from what you perceive when you are a missionary or a mother or father. In other words, as you occupy different roles in your life, you will come to view blessings in ways that apply to you at that time.

# COUNT YOUR BLESSINGS

So, first of all, go through your patriarchal blessing and inventory all the different blessings that you have been given, including your lineage. Where much is given, much gratitude is expected. Do you need to express gratitude to your parents? Do you praise them and thank them for all that they have done? Do you thank them and your leaders in the Church for teaching you the gospel? Some people are converts and may not have the blessing of parents who can teach them the principles of the restored gospel of Jesus Christ—but they have Heavenly Parents. Should we not all be grateful for Them and for our Savior Jesus Christ? In other words, you can gratefully use your patriarchal blessing as a window looking out upon your future. With thanksgiving, you can ponder all the things that you can accomplish through each one of your blessings or gifts—things that will bring happiness to you, your family, and others whose lives you might be able to influence for good.

Oftentimes future blessings are mentioned, blessings of Abraham, Isaac, and Jacob, or blessings of eternal life. Now, when you look in the scriptures and see what Abraham, Isaac, and Jacob are now doing, you will note in Doctrine and Covenants 132:37 that they are no longer angels in the heavenly realm but are in truth, gods. Your blessings are predicated upon your faithfulness, so in order to receive the blessings of Abraham, Isaac, and Jacob, you will need to rise up and live the kind of life that will allow you to follow in the footsteps of the prophets and of the Savior.

What does it take to become a just man or woman? It means we have to live by faith in the atoning sacrifice. As explained in the Doctrine and Covenants, "These are they whose names are written in heaven, where God and Christ are the judge of all. These are they who are just men made perfect through Jesus the mediator of the new covenant, who wrought out this perfect atonement through the shedding of his own blood" (D&C 76:68–69).

So as you live by faith and do every needful thing, you can become perfect. You can receive the blessings of exaltation. You can receive the blessings of Abraham, Isaac, and Jacob—to come forth in the morning of the first resurrection. What a blessing in your life to know that you can be saved if you are obedient to the commandments of God! Carefully go through your entire patriarchal blessing to enumerate your blessings and your gifts, and then write down your plans to have them become a reality in your life.

## RECEIVE ADMONITIONS WITH THANKSGIVING

Next, look for the admonitions in your patriarchal blessing. You may be encouraged to do many things. For example, you might be encouraged to pray often. If so, that is what you need to do. You can cross-reference the advice given in your blessing with the scriptures. As an example, here is what the scriptures tell us about the importance of praying:

Yea, cry unto him for mercy; for he is mighty to save.

Yea, humble yourselves, and continue in prayer unto him.

Cry unto him when ye are in your fields, yea, over all your flocks.

Cry unto him in your houses, yea, over all your household, both morning, mid-day, and evening.

Yea, cry unto him against the power of your enemies.

Yea, cry unto him against the devil, who is an enemy to all righteousness.

Cry unto him over the crops of your fields, that ye may prosper in them.

Cry over the flocks of your fields, that they may increase.

But this is not all; ye must pour out your souls in your closets, and your secret places, and in your wilderness.

Yea, and when you do not cry unto the Lord, let your hearts be full, drawn out in prayer unto him continually for your welfare, and also for the welfare of those who are around you.

And now behold, my beloved brethren, I say unto you, do not suppose that this is all; for after ye have done all these things, if ye turn away the needy, and the naked, and visit not the sick and afflicted, and impart of your substance, if ye have, to those who stand in need—I say unto you, if ye do not any of these things, behold,

your prayer is vain, and availeth you nothing,
and ye are as hypocrites who do deny the faith.
(Alma 34:18–28)

Consider all of the things you should pray for.
Prayer is a mighty shield against temptation: "Behold,
verily, verily, I say unto you, ye must watch and pray
always lest ye enter into temptation; for Satan desireth
to have you, that he may sift you as wheat" (3 Nephi
18:18). By praying sincerely and regularly, you will
have greater ability to withstand temptation. As you
approach your Father in Heaven in prayer, you should
ask for His blessings, and He will bless you according
to your worthiness. So if your patriarchal blessing
admonishes you to pray, you have a wonderful opportunity to follow the Lord's counsel by asking in faith,
with real intent, that you might receive His guidance
and blessings.

If you are encouraged to be exactly obedient, you
should then learn that obedience is the first law of
heaven. If you are admonished to obey and then have
an inclination to say, "Well, but I won't do this or I
won't do that," you are setting aside the word of the
Lord and forfeiting the blessings that come through
obedience. Remember, if you obey and keep the commandments, you can enjoy the state of happiness
described by King Benjamin:

And moreover, I would desire that ye should
consider on the blessed and happy state of those
that keep the commandments of God. For

behold, they are blessed in all things, both temporal and spiritual; and if they hold out faithful to the end they are received into heaven, that thereby they may dwell with God in a state of never-ending happiness. O remember, remember that these things are true; for the Lord God hath spoken it. (Mosiah 2:41)

All of God's children can receive the blessings of eternal happiness by being obedient and keeping His commandments. So it is important for you to make a list of all that you are admonished, encouraged, or exhorted to do in your patriarchal blessing. As you make this list, write on the right side of the page the things you plan to do in each case to be obedient. If your blessing says to pray, then pray morning, noon, and night. Keep a prayer in your heart throughout the day. If your blessing encourages you to listen to the still, small voice of the Spirit, then remain in tune with the Spirit through obedience and cultivating pure thoughts and behavior. If your blessing says that you should follow your priesthood leaders, then heed their counsel and advice at all times. All these things can make a difference in your life as you follow the Lord's counsel.

Oftentimes in a patriarchal blessing, the Lord will say "beware," or "remember," or "don't forget." These cautions should remind you to do what is right. For example, if the Lord were to say, "Seek out good companions," that means just what it says: you should associate with good people who make good choices.

You should associate with friends who choose the right. If you put yourself in compromising situations, you could be accused of something you had no part in. Because you made a choice to be in the wrong place at the wrong time with the wrong people and you didn't listen to the caution of your patriarchal blessing, you could suffer dire consequences. On the other hand, by carefully seeking out only the best companions, those who live the gospel teachings, you will enjoy wonderful, uplifting blessings of the Spirit.

Carefully write down each caution or concern that is mentioned in your patriarchal blessing. After you write it down, explain on the right side of the page any specific actions you feel impressed to record: "Be at the right place at the right time." "Always attend my church meetings." "Stay close to family and good friends." In other words, highlight the cautions as things to be aware of, and then write down positive things to do to be sure that you adhere to such counsel. In that way, you can be safe and protected through the Lord's guidance.

When you follow the counsel in your patriarchal blessing—when you read it, study it, live it, and apply it to your life—the blessings of heaven and the blessings of eternal life can be yours. Nephi expresses this promise in these inspiring words: "Wherefore, ye must press forward with a steadfastness in Christ, having a perfect brightness of hope, and a love of God and of all men. Wherefore, if ye shall press forward, feasting upon the word of Christ, and endure to the end, behold, thus saith the Father: Ye shall have eternal life" (2 Ne. 31:20).

All of these things are imperative to ensure that your patriarchal blessing is fulfilled in your lifetime and in the life to come. Look at the blessings mentioned in the message given to you through the patriarch and make a list of them. Make a commitment concerning the positive things you should do to receive those blessings. Make a commitment to keep *all* of the commandments of the Lord so that His promised blessings can flow into your life, based on the personal revelation given in your patriarchal blessing.

# THINGS TO REMEMBER CONCERNING YOUR PATRIARCHAL BLESSING

As you read and reread your patriarchal blessing, remember that it is just for you. Look at the words the patriarch has given to you by inspiration, and prayerfully focus on the marvelous things that you have been told. Avoid looking "beyond the mark" (Jacob 4:14). You should avoid reading things into your blessing that are not there. Look at the blessing in regard to your life, and make a commitment to become more righteous. The purpose of the patriarchal blessing is to help you on your path to eternal life, and righteousness is the key to exaltation.

# SAVOR THE JOY OF
## YOUR PATRIARCHAL BLESSING

You recall in the dream of Lehi that the fruit of the tree of life was delicious and most satisfying (see 1 Ne. 8:11). This tree and its fruit represent something very special: "Yea, it is the love of God, which sheddeth itself abroad in the hearts of the children of men; wherefore, it is the most desirable above all things" (1 Ne. 11:22). This is a tree "whose fruit is most precious and most desirable above all other fruits; yea, and it is the greatest of all the gifts of God" (1 Ne. 15:36).

In a similar way, your patriarchal blessing is a most desirable fruit, because it is given to you as a manifestation of the love of God. It is part of the "bread of life" that the Savior spoke about (see John 6:35, 48). It is also akin to the well of living water that the Savior referred to while speaking to the Samaritan woman (see John 4:14). Partaking of such bread and water will satisfy one's hunger and thirst forever, because these are the nutrients of the gospel of Jesus Christ provided through the Atonement. Your patriarchal blessing is part of the banquet of everlasting life that the Savior offers to you and to all of His sons and daughters. Should we not all be grateful that Heavenly Father and His Son provide such marvelous gifts and blessings to us to lift us up and help us to be better people?

Now, just think, you know that Heavenly Father loves you and cares for you. He seeks to help you personally. He has specific things for you to do to help you in your life here upon the earth. Remember, as you proceed in life, your perceptions will change and your view of your patriarchal blessing will change, just as it does when you read the scriptures at different times. From time to time, you may see things in the scriptures that you have missed before, simply because your situation is evolving and the Spirit may point out to you precisely what you need to be doing and thinking about for your salvation.

Similarly, your patriarchal blessing will become more meaningful to you the longer you live. Come to an understanding of and an appreciation for all that God has done for you, all that His magnificent plan provides—the opportunity to prepare to meet Him personally and the way to exaltation and eternal life. Remember that receiving a personal blessing from God is a special privilege. He will surely be pleased as you hearken to the words in your patriarchal blessing and enjoy the blessings of exaltation through obedience to His commandments.

# FREQUENTLY ASKED QUESTIONS

*Why is lineage so important in my blessing?*
The blessings of Abraham, Isaac, and Jacob—the House of Israel—entitle one to great promises from our Heavenly Father. There are blessings and responsibilities that come through the lineage of Father Abraham including the privilege of carrying the gospel to every nation, kindred, tongue, and people. Here is the marvelous blessing that the Lord gave to Abraham:

My name is Jehovah, and I know the end from the beginning; therefore my hand shall be over thee.

And I will make of thee a great nation, and I will bless thee above measure, and make thy name great among all nations, and thou shalt be a blessing unto thy seed after thee, that in their hands they shall bear this ministry and Priesthood unto all nations;

And I will bless them through thy name; for as many as receive this Gospel shall be called after thy name, and shall be accounted thy seed, and shall rise up and bless thee, as their father;

And I will bless them that bless thee, and curse them that curse thee; and in thee (that is, in thy Priesthood) and in thy seed (that is, thy Priesthood), for I give unto thee a promise that this right shall continue in thee, and in thy seed after thee (that is to say, the literal seed, or the seed of the body) shall all the families of the earth be blessed, even with the blessings of the Gospel, which are the blessings of salvation, even of life eternal. (Abr. 2:8–11)

Think of it! Because you are part of this noble lineage, you have the opportunity to be a leader in building up the kingdom of God and taking the gospel message to your friends and colleagues at home and abroad. This lineage brings magnificent blessings into your life. Father in Heaven wants you to be happy and have joy—hence, He has established a way for grand blessings to flow to you for your faithful service. Your lineage is the channel through which these blessings can flow. You can be grateful that our Father in Heaven and His Son know you personally and want you to grow and follow in the footsteps of righteousness. That is why your patriarchal blessing is so important—because it shows you the way to receive the blessings of exaltation through your faithfulness in living up to those responsibilities.

*Should I share my blessings with others?*

Your patriarchal blessing is sacred. You should take special care to regard it as a personal and private document, sharing it only with special loved ones or, on occasion, with Church leaders from whom you seek advice. Remember—your blessing is never to be compared with the blessings of others. It is your own special blessing from your Heavenly Father.

*Is my patriarchal blessing for this earth life only?*

Sometimes patriarchal blessings include references to pre-earth life and life after death in addition to our mortal experience here and now. Your blessing is not necessarily limited only to mortality. It may include possibilities for all phases of your life.

*Does my patriarchal blessing tell me everything I will ever do here upon the earth?*

No. A patriarchal blessing gives direction. It is a compass for your life. It is your Liahona. It can give you advice and counsel and general direction. But it is not intended to give you direction regarding every aspect of your life. It is not fortune telling. It gives direction, admonition, encouragement, and cautions.

# How to Apply Your Patriarchal Blessing to Your Daily Life

*Be ambitious to be great, not in the estimation of the worldly*

*minded, but in the eyes of God.*

—Lorenzo Snow

# YOUR COMPASS OF TRUTH

Once you have received your patriarchal blessing, your life will never be the same. You will have the privilege of following counsel and revelation given to you directly from the Lord. Your life will change and develop as you apply your patriarchal blessing with faith and thanksgiving.

There are six specific things you may wish to consider day by day as you allow your patriarchal blessing to be a compass for your life to help you to always be true to the standards of the gospel:

1. Realize your potential. Know that you are a son or daughter of God, with a divine potential to become like Him and His Only Begotten Son.

2. Rejoice over your gifts and blessings. Gratefully thank Heavenly Father for these marvelous blessings in your life.

3. Follow the counsel and admonitions given.

4. Listen to the warnings and cautions given.

5. View yourself as an important part of the lineage of Israel, with the great opportunity to help spread the gospel of Jesus Christ.

6. Look forward in joy and faith to the fulfillment of your patriarchal blessing, based on your obedience and righteousness.

Let us consider each of these six key points and identify what you might do each day to bring about the fulfillment of your patriarchal blessing.

## REALIZE YOUR POTENTIAL

Examine the descriptions, attributes, and qualities that may have been mentioned in your blessing and seek to become in full measure the glorious person presented in this spiritual portrait of your potential.

*Some Examples*

Perhaps a young woman might find wording in her patriarchal blessing that ascribes to her the following kinds of qualities: being charitable (having a disposition to be kind at all times to others), showing leadership (with reference to future positions of service among the Saints), motherhood (with the promise of bringing children into the world and nurturing them in love), and valor (being able to endure to the end in righteousness by overcoming life's challenges and temptations). Such qualities would then become beacons of light toward which this young woman would be drawn as she followed through with the commitment to fulfill these choice promises.

Perhaps a young man might find reference to the following kinds of attributes and characteristics in his patriarchal blessing: loyalty in emulating the example of his righteous forebears and ancestors, discernment in understanding and responding effectively to the needs of his fellow beings as a counselor and guide, strength to overcome temptation through the power of prayer, and wisdom in finding a worthy young woman to be his eternal mate. Wouldn't this young man seek diligently to foster such qualities as he progressed day by day toward greater spiritual maturity and development? Just knowing that the seeds of greatness for such qualities were part of his nature as a son of God would allow him to cultivate those seeds carefully and tend with devotion his growth and progress.

Perhaps a convert to the Church might find reference in her patriarchal blessing to such attributes as nobility (rising in stature and spirituality to take her place among the Saints of God), understanding (as in the ability to derive light and truth from the holy scriptures), patience in learning God's plan of salvation, and faith in coming to view herself as a daughter of her Heavenly Father, with the potential of receiving all the blessings and glory reserved for the righteous and valiant of Zion. Would this convert not feel edified and rejoice in such glorious promises received as a personal revelation from the Lord?

Whatever qualities, attributes, and talents you might find mentioned in your patriarchal blessing, you can know that these have been given to you by a loving Father in Heaven who knows you very well from the premortal existence. You may have cultivated these very qualities for a long while *before* you came to this earth. In a way, you might be on a journey to rediscover them and apply them for good in serving the needs of your family and others while in this phase of your life. It is also possible that Heavenly Father has granted you special new talents and gifts for specific reasons that have to do with your coming roles on earth as a leader, a parent, or a missionary of the gospel. It is up to you to cultivate and apply the talents and gifts the Lord has granted you "that all may be profited thereby" (D&C 46:12). Above all, you should strive to develop the qualities that are exemplified by Heavenly Father and His Son Jesus Christ. Here is how President Lorenzo Snow described this wonderful process of "becoming":

> Be upright, just, and merciful, exercising a spirit of nobility and godliness in all your intentions and resolutions—in all your acts and dealings. Cultivate a spirit of charity, be ready to do for others more than you would expect from them if circumstances were reversed. Be ambitious to be great, not in the estimation of the worldly minded, but in the eyes of God, and to be great in this sense: "Love the Lord your God with all your might, mind and strength, and your neighbor as yourself." You must love mankind because they are your brethren, the offspring of God. Pray diligently for this spirit of philanthropy,

this expansion of thought and feeling, and for power and ability to labor earnestly in the interest of Messiah's kingdom. (*The Teachings of Lorenzo Snow,*1984, 10)

*Ideas to Help You Reach Your Potential*

The following ideas will help you become the great person you find reflected in your patriarchal blessing—someone who shows the qualities of godliness a little more each day.

- Ponder the word of God. Study God's word as given in the scriptures and through the voice of the living prophets. In the scriptures and the messages of our current prophet, the attributes of godliness are identified, clarified, and presented for your emulation (see Jacob 3:2; Alma 32:28; D&C 138:1–11).

- Choose the best patterns. Organize and structure your life after the best models and examples, including the Lord's prophets and servants, your family members, and your righteous neighbors and friends. Especially seek to follow in the footsteps of the Savior (see Matt. 16:24).

- Be pure. Cleanliness is next to godliness as reflected in purity of thought (see Prov. 23:7) and actions (see James 1:22; Mosiah 5:15).

- Be obedient. Godliness entails righteousness (see D&C 27:16; 98:30). Faith is the foundation of righteousness (see Rom. 3:22; 9:30–32). Thus you can seek godliness through your faith and righteous devotion (see 2 Pet. 1:3–12; Moro. 10:32–33; D&C 4:6).

- Be a leader in all walks of life. Godliness involves being a good example. Through your example you can lift and bless others (see 1 Tim. 4:12; Alma 17:11; 3 Ne. 12:16).

- Be prepared. Recognize that those who lead a godly life will likely suffer persecution in one form or another (see 2 Tim. 3:12). Understand the blessings and the challenges that come from persecution and sacrifice.

- Remember each day. Come up with ways to remind yourself to continually strive to develop the attributes of godliness. Surround yourself with reminders (pictures, charts, posters, notes, wall and table ornaments—anything that will bring the principles of godliness to mind throughout the day). Guard against forgetting due to the ease of the way (see Hel. 12:1–2); instead, remember the goodness and mercy of the Lord in all things (see Mosiah 4:11).

## REJOICE OVER YOUR GIFTS AND BLESSINGS

Receive with joy and gratitude the promised blessings that may have been revealed to you through the patriarch. Live in such a manner that these blessings can be granted to the full extent, based on your faithfulness and devotion. The prophet Joseph F. Smith expressed the following thought about gratitude:

> The grateful man sees so much in the world to be thankful for, and with him the good outweighs the evil. Love overpowers jealousy, and light drives darkness out of his life. Pride destroys our gratitude and sets up selfishness in its place. How much happier we are in the presence of a grateful and loving soul, and how careful we should be to cultivate, through the medium of a prayerful life, a thankful attitude toward God and man! (*Gospel Doctrine: Selections from the Sermons and Writings of Joseph F. Smith,* 1998, 263)

*Some Examples*

Let us suppose that one young man learned from his patriarchal blessing that he would one day become a father in Zion, with children who would rise up and call his name blessed. Would he not look forward in gratitude to the time when this blessing would become reality? Would he not wish to prepare for that day by cultivating what the Lord calls "a godly walk and conversation" (D&C 20:69)—in other words, by keeping the commandments and living worthy of the Spirit? Would this young man not have in his mind at all times the desire to be a good example to his children so that they, in very fact, would one day express to him their thanks for his righteous pattern of living?

Think of a young woman who might learn in her patriarchal blessing that she would one day occupy a place of honor among the leading sisters of the Church. Would she not look forward with joy in contemplating how that might come about? Would she not strive to gain the qualities of leadership that might enable her to serve in such a capacity with dignity and success? Would she not be thankful that the Lord, in His infinite wisdom, had seen in her the potential to help build His kingdom in specific ways and at specific times? And as her opportunities for service were realized, one after the other, would she not rejoice to recall through the Spirit that she was fulfilling a personal revelation given to her through one of the Lord's choice servants? Such is the nature and power of a patriarchal blessing.

Think of a convert to the Church coming into the fold as an adult who might find in his patriarchal blessing a reference to his being one of the saviors on Mount Zion (see Obadiah 1:21), called to complete temple work for countless of his ancestors who were waiting in the spirit world for this very service to be accomplished. Would he not rejoice at the opportunity to perform such honorable and worthy service in the temples of the Most High? Would he not cultivate a pattern of living that would reflect faith and virtue and righteousness so that he could benefit from the guidance of the Spirit in doing family history work and bringing an accurate record of his progenitors to the house of the Lord?

Whatever blessings and promises the Lord might provide for you in His generosity and love, you can look forward in gratitude to the opportunity of rising to your heaven-given potential as a child of God.

*Ideas to Help You Cultivate and Show Gratitude for Your Gifts and Blessings*

Here are several things you can do to understand and show gratitude for the things that Heavenly Father has given you or promised to give you:

- Remember that gratitude spreads under its own power. When you are grateful to Heavenly Father and everyone around you, this attitude becomes contagious and spreads to family, community, and society, neutralizing envy, jealousy, and anger.

- Remember that gratitude brings its own rewards. When you show gratitude to Heavenly Father for your blessings, you become more at peace, closer to family and friends, more radiant and self-confident, a better leader, and more worthy of the blessings of the Spirit (see Gal. 5:22–23; D&C 11:12–13).

- Remember that gratitude starts with the little things. Look around and open your vision to the good in things and look for the best in others. Often by just looking for things to be grateful for, you will find that you have blessings in abundance. And you will discover at the same time that there are always people who have more trials and problems than you do. Count your many blessings. Notice others doing good. By noticing others doing good and expressing gratitude to them, you open the way for greater happiness and joy in life. It's all too easy to see the negative, but it takes a strong spirit to see the positive and be grateful for it.

- Keep the commandment to be thankful. The Lord expects us all to feel and express thanksgiving and gratitude. We are to thank God in all things (see Eph. 5:20). We offend God when we fail to give thanks (see Mosiah 26:39, D&C 59:21). Therefore, learn to receive all things with thanksgiving—especially your patriarchal blessing. When you receive things with thanksgiving to your God, you will be exceedingly blessed (see Mosiah 2:19–21; D&C 78:19). Fill your prayers with gratitude to the Lord (see Amos 4:5; 1 Ne. 2:7; 5:9). Your true offering of thanksgiving and gratitude can be the sacrifice of your whole soul for the cause of the Lord (see Omni 1:26)—doing all that He has asked of you.

## FOLLOW THE COUNSEL AND ADMONITIONS GIVEN

Willingly follow the counsel and guidance given in your patriarchal blessing. Let your blessing serve as a spiritual compass for your life, marking clearly the guiding line down the middle of the straight and narrow path of righteousness. Following that line takes a willingness to learn from God. It takes being teachable and humble. President Spencer W. Kimball has said:

How does one get humble? To me, one must constantly be reminded of his dependence. On whom dependent? On the Lord. How to remind one's self? By real, constant, worshipful, grateful prayer. . . .

Humility is teachableness—an ability to realize that all virtues and abilities are not concentrated in one's self. . . .

Humility is gracious, quiet, serene—not pompous, spectacular, nor histrionic. It is subdued, kindly, and understanding—not crude, blatant, loud, or ugly. Humility is not just a man or a woman but a perfect gentleman and a gentlelady. It never struts nor swaggers. Its faithful, quiet works will be the badge of its own accomplishments. It never sets itself in the center of the stage, leaving all others in supporting roles. Humility is never accusing nor contentious. It is not boastful. . . .

Humility is repentant and seeks not to justify its follies. It is forgiving others in the realization that there may be errors of the same kind or worse chalked up against itself. . . .

It is not self-abasement—the hiding in the corner, the devaluation of everything one does or thinks or says; but it is the doing of one's best in every case and leaving of one's acts, expressions, and accomplishments to largely speak for themselves. (*The Teachings of Spencer W. Kimball*, 1982, 233)

## Some Examples

Think of a convert to the Church who might find a reference in his patriarchal blessing to the need to heed carefully the whisperings of the still, small voice. Would he not wish to learn through study and prayer how to tune his heart and mind to be sensitive to the Spirit? Would he not take steps to tune out the noise and clamor of worldly influences—whether from shallow or impure television shows, the negative and harmful aspects of the Internet, questionable music or literature, or so-called friends who would try to lead him astray? Would he not heed the advice of the living prophets and study the scriptures to understand the process of personal inspiration? Would he not seek out and choose only the most uplifting and appropriate forms of entertainment and media? Would he not listen carefully and humbly to the promptings of the Holy Ghost as a guide and influence along the way? What a choice blessing to be able to follow the Lord through the whisperings of the Holy Ghost!

Let's suppose a young woman was counseled in her patriarchal blessing to choose her friends carefully, that she might remain within the fold of the Savior and not stray into hidden pathways and dark byways. Would she not have these words in mind every time she was invited by friends to go and participate in activities? Would she not view her associates through the lens of spirituality in deciding the course for her future relationships? Would she not prayerfully seek to form friendships with those who honor their covenants and reflect a life based on high standards? Because of this aspect of her patriarchal blessing, this young woman might well make the decision once and for all—ahead of time—to restrict her close friendships to people who were near to the Lord. That would not mean that she could not continue to be a good example to everyone and to reflect kindness and charity to those who might be struggling. But what a blessing it would be to her if she surrounded herself with valiant sons and daughters of God who would be a powerful support group to her in living the commandments and following in the footsteps of the Savior. In this way, her patriarchal blessing truly would be a prophecy of her ultimate triumph as a faithful daughter of God, destined to be joyfully secure in the arms of the Master.

Let's suppose a young man was counseled in his patriarchal blessing to strive for balance in his life, always remembering to put God and family first. Would this young man not have this advice always in his mind as he pursued his career choices? Would he not put selfish interests in check and strive to be more charitable and service minded? Would he not look forward to the time when he might be a husband and father and demonstrate through his devotion to his family that he remembers the counsel of God? Would he not respond more willingly to the various stewardship calls that might come to him through priesthood channels? Would he not prayerfully seek God's help in being wise and balanced in his decisions? In such a way, his patriarchal blessing could serve as a framework for future decision making based on eternal principles and spiritual ideals for living.

*Ideas for Becoming More Teachable and Humble*

Here are several ideas to help you follow the advice and counsel given to you in your patriarchal blessing:

- Remember that humility is the beginning of spirituality. Therefore, fast and pray to be humble and open to the Lord's counsel (see Hel. 3:35). Cultivate a broken heart. "The Lord is nigh unto them that are of a broken heart; and saveth such as be of a contrite spirit" (Ps. 34:18). Listen to spiritual input so that you can always be learning and progressing (see Alma 13:28). Recognize and remember your relationship to God and your total dependence upon Him (see Mosiah 4:5).

- Remember that to be humble is to be strong. Humility is a quality of strength (see Hel. 3:35), for it says of an individual that he or she is willing to learn, willing to heed the counsel of God, and willing to admit mistakes and go on to improve. Therefore, as you read and reread your patriarchal blessing, be willing to learn from it. Be clothed in humility in everything you do and say (see 1 Pet. 5:5).

- Show humility in the family. Let family members help you apply the great promises and guidance in your patriarchal blessing. Let them be resources to support you in fulfilling the Lord's counsel to you. Grow together. Be happy together. Find joy in the gospel of Jesus Christ. Respect one another. Be good examples, kind and courteous and gracious.

# LISTEN TO THE WARNINGS AND CAUTIONS GIVEN

Where specific cautions might be given relative to the course of your life, prayerfully heed this divine guidance and warning. Let your blessing be a beacon of truth and a lighthouse of wisdom to expose any hidden reefs of danger and illuminate the course of safety through the shoals of life. President Harold B. Lee expressed the need for us to heed the warning signals from our Heavenly Father:

> It's an interesting thing that sometimes it takes calamity to drive us together. It's a terrifying thing to think that that's necessary, but the Lord said through one of His prophets that sometimes we have to have the chastening hand of the Almighty before we will wake up and humble ourselves to do the thing that He has asked us to do (see Hel. 12:3–6). In talking about the conditions that would come, He warned the people that death and destruction and all sorts of difficulties would have to come before people would listen, before they would obey, and He removes His hand and lets these things occur, or our people would not repent and come unto the Lord. (*The Teachings of Harold B. Lee*, 1998, 191)

Moreover, James E. Faust has provided this choice counsel concerning ways for us to navigate the sometimes complex and bumpy roadways of life:

President Howard W. Hunter once said, "God knows what we do not know and sees what we do not see." None of us knows the wisdom of the Lord. We do not know in advance exactly how He would get us from where we are to where we need to be, but He does offer us broad outlines in our patriarchal blessings. We encounter many bumps, bends, and forks in the road of life that leads to the eternities. There is so much teaching and correction as we travel on that road. Said the Lord, "He that will not bear chastisement is not worthy of my kingdom." "For whom the Lord loveth he chasteneth." ("Where Do I Make My Stand?" *Ensign*, Nov. 2004, 21)

## Some Examples

Suppose that a young man received counsel in his patriarchal blessing that he should follow the Lord's law of health, implying that he should take care to eat a wholesome, balanced diet and avoid harmful substances that would be destructive to his health. Would he not be inclined to establish healthful eating patterns and to avoid tobacco, alcohol, illicit drugs, and all other substances that the Lord has warned us against? Would he not be impressed to stay clear of environments and social circles where the use of such harmful substances was encouraged? The Lord has characterized the body in the following way: "Know ye not that ye are the temple of God, and that the Spirit of God dwelleth in you? If any man defile the temple of God, him shall God destroy; for the temple of God is holy, which temple ye are" (1 Cor. 3:16–17). At the same time, this young man could derive from his patriarchal blessing a very special and personal feeling of appreciation for the promises given by the Lord for those who heed the Word of Wisdom:

And all saints who remember to keep and do these sayings, walking in obedience to the com mandments, shall receive health in their navel and marrow to their bones;

And shall find wisdom and great treasures of knowledge, even hidden treasures;

And shall run and not be weary, and shall walk and not faint.

And I, the Lord, give unto them a promise, that the destroying angel shall pass by them, as the children of Israel, and not slay them. (D&C 89:18–21)

We might think of a young woman whose patriarchal blessing counseled her to aspire to a life of virtue and cleanliness, assuring her that the Lord would give her the strength to transcend and defeat the temptations of mortality if she would heed the inspiration of the Spirit. Would she not be watchful in holding to the iron rod and avoiding all circumstances that could compromise her standards as a daughter of God? Would her patriarchal blessing not serve as a source of light to illuminate before her the straight and narrow path of righteousness and purity? What a blessing to know that Heavenly Father would watch over her and give her the strength to triumph as a valiant follower of the Savior. Would this young woman not have special appreciation for the words of the prophet Alma, where he stated:

> But that ye would humble yourselves before the Lord, and call on his holy name, and watch and pray continually, that ye may not be tempted above that which ye can bear, and thus be led by the Holy Spirit, becoming humble, meek, submissive, patient, full of love and all long-suffering;
>
> Having faith on the Lord; having a hope that ye shall receive eternal life; having the love of God always in your hearts, that ye may be lifted up at the last day and enter into his rest. (Alma 13:28–29)

Finally, let us suppose that a middle-aged convert was counseled in his patriarchal blessing to avoid pride, always cultivating a broken heart and a spirit of humility and gratitude. Do you suppose that this man would not find special relevance in the Book of Mormon accounts of how great nations succumbed to pride and selfishness through self-centered neglect of gospel principles? Would he not find comfort and encouragement to read about the spiritual blossoming of those—like King Benjamin's followers, or the congregation assembled about Alma the Elder at the Waters of Mormon, or the faithful Saints instructed by the resurrected Savior—who came unto the Lord in meekness, being easily entreated and counseled? In this way, this convert's patriarchal blessing would serve as a powerful antidote to pride, and a protection from the winds of arrogance and selfishness.

*Ideas to Help You Heed the Warnings in Your Patriarchal Blessing*

Here are several things you can do to prepare yourself to listen to and follow the cautions, warnings, and admonitions in your patriarchal blessing.

- Perceive the love behind Heavenly Father's warnings. Recognize that if He warns you through the patriarch, He is doing so to spare you future pain and anguish. He knows you very well—your strengths and weaknesses—and wants you to be happy. Thus, He might set forth warning signs along the way so that you can avoid danger and stay safe and secure.

- Be watchful. Take the Lord's counsel seriously and practice patience in following His counsel and watching for the warning signs. The Lord sees everything far better than we can see for ourselves. Therefore, is it not wise to see things through His eyes and follow the words given in your patriarchal blessing?

- Remember the specific warnings. Put up little notes or reminders where you can see them every day. For example, if the Lord instructs you to choose your friends very carefully, then put up a poster on friendship or wear a little pin that will remind you to make wise choices.

# VIEW YOURSELF AS AN IMPORTANT PART OF THE LINEAGE OF ISRAEL

Give praise to the Lord that He has anchored you securely within the fold of His covenant people and revealed to you your lineage and responsibility to it. Give thanks that you can serve with devotion to help build the kingdom of God and carry the message of deliverance and salvation to many others in keeping with the obligations and responsibilities of the Abrahamic covenant. Be grateful that the patriarch has declared the tribe of Israel through which your covenant blessings will flow, based on your faithfulness and obedience. The Savior said:

> And behold, ye are the children of the prophets; and ye are of the house of Israel; and ye are of the covenant which the Father made with your fathers, saying unto Abraham: And in thy seed shall all the kindreds of the earth be blessed.
> The Father having raised me up unto you first, and sent me to bless you in turning away every one of you from his iniquities; and this because ye are the children of the covenant. (3 Nephi 20:25–26)

In this regard, James E. Faust has declared, "If you keep the covenants and commandments of God, you will have the joy promised by the Savior when he walked upon the earth. You will have 'peace in this world, and eternal life in the world to come' (D&C 59:23)" (*Reach Up for the Light*, 1990, 69).

*Some Examples*

The hearts of many young men and women in the Church hold the seeds of missionary work. Through careful preparation and goal setting, these young men and women emerge from their formative years ready and willing to serve in building the kingdom of God.

Let us suppose that a young man finds in his patriarchal blessing a marvelous promise that, being of the House of Israel (a specific tribe being mentioned), he would in due time be called forth to carry the gospel with great power and authority to the waiting peoples of the earth and that the harvest of grateful souls would be not a few. Would he not prepare more earnestly, with greater devotion, to fulfill this personal revelation from the Lord? Would he not feast upon the scriptures and keep his life in tune with the Spirit in order to be fully worthy of a mission call? Surely a promise of this kind, conveyed through a patriarchal blessing, would serve as a compass directing this young man toward the heavenly priesthood objective of becoming one of the Lord's appointed servants.

Think of a couple who joined the Church in their middle years. The time for a youthful mission call was past, but what if each of them were privileged to obtain patriarchal blessings and learn, among many other things, that the Lord had in mind for them a future opportunity to spread the gospel through missionary service? Would they not begin immediately to prepare themselves for such service in the due time of the Lord? Would they not rejoice to think that they too would be blessed to fulfill their role in carrying out an important aspect of the Abrahamic covenant by sharing the gospel with others? What a comfort such a patriarchal blessing would be to these converts.

Let us suppose that a young woman received a patriarchal blessing in which she learned that she was of the tribe of Ephraim, entitled to all of the blessings reserved by the Lord for such. Would she not study the scriptures and counsel with her family and priesthood leaders about this noble heritage? Would she not want to learn more about Abraham, Isaac, and Jacob? Would she not be interested in learning about the patriarchal blessings that Israel bestowed upon his sons (recorded in Genesis 49), in particular upon Joseph (father of Ephraim)? Would this young woman not find inspiration in understanding that she was entitled to participate in these same blessings associated with the noble cause of carrying the gospel "unto all nations" (Abr. 2:9), even should she not serve as a full-time missionary in her youth? Perhaps she would carry the gospel to her neighbors through her example and kindness. Perhaps she would come to know that her future children would become faithful emissaries of the Lord under the inspiration of her instruction. In these ways, her patriarchal blessing might extend its influence over many years—even decades—as a road map leading to eternal life for herself, her family, and many other faithful sons and daughters of God.

*Ideas for Honoring Your Lineage and Heritage as a Son or Daughter of the Covenant*

Here are several ideas you can apply as you ponder and think about your lineage as one of the "children of the covenant" (3 Ne. 20:26):

- Understand and appreciate your covenants. Study carefully the doctrines, principles, ordinances, and covenants of the Church by searching the scriptures and the words of our living prophets (see D&C 21:4–6; 84:43–45).

- Pray for an understanding of how you fit into the Lord's plan for His covenant people. Knowledge comes from our Heavenly Father by the Holy Spirit. He can reveal to you eternal truths that bring a comprehension of those things you seek to know, understand, and appreciate (see Prov. 3:5; Alma 17:2). You may need to pray often for the ability to accept things on faith; by doing so, you will surely receive a witness that they are true, for the Lord has promised it (see Ether 12:6; Moro. 10:4–5). As a result, you will be filled with gratitude, which will give you a desire to keep your covenants.

- Keep your covenants. Jesus taught that we can come to know the truth of the gospel primarily by living the doctrines and commandments of God (see John 7:17). We can and will receive the blessings of eternal life by keeping our covenants and enduring to the end (see 2 Ne. 33:4; D&C 101:38–40). Your patriarchal blessing is one of the important tools to help you endure to the end in harmony with the principles of the gospel of Jesus Christ.

- Participate in temple activities. For example, you can take part in baptisms for the dead so that you can deepen your understanding of the Lord's magnificent blessing to His covenant people. Revelation concerning many truths can come as we seek enlightenment within the walls of the house of the Lord (see D&C 97:13–16). As you mature in the gospel, you can look forward to partaking of other blessings that are available in the temples of God.

- Plan to remember. An active system for remembering is the key to not forgetting your covenant promises. Sometimes it is easy to forget due to the busyness of life and the ease of the way (see Hel. 12:2–3). For example, the Lord has given us the sacrament as a weekly reminder to stay focused on the gospel plan. You can use your own ingenuity to add a variety of simple memory aids to your daily life: a sign, a note, a helpful reminder from a friend. Such simple things can awaken within you a remembrance of your covenant promises.

- Exercise your faith. In faith, all things can and will be done (see Moro. 7:33). Remember, faith moves you to action and gives the power to do all things. Your patriarchal blessing is a significant exercise in faith.

- Write a mission statement. Your mission statement could include references to your lineage as declared in your patriarchal blessing, as well as to the commitments of obedience you have made through baptism. You can make reference to the great spiritual benefits that will flow to you through your lineage, based on your faithfulness and valor. Take the time to review your mission statement on a regular basis. With such a renewed emphasis, you will become stronger in the process of keeping your covenants with honor and exactness.

## LOOK FORWARD IN JOY AND FAITH TO THE FULFILLMENT OF YOUR PATRIARCHAL BLESSING, BASED ON YOUR OBEDIENCE AND RIGHTEOUSNESS

There are wonderful blessings that will come to you as you fulfill the promises and admonitions in your patriarchal blessing. View your patriarchal blessing as a spiritual passport to the realization of divine promises that the Lord, in His mercy and loving kindness, has bestowed upon you *personally* through one of

His chosen priesthood servants. A righteous heart will always draw the blessings of the Spirit. Brigham Young has said:

> Every son and daughter of God is expected to obey with a willing heart every word which the Lord has spoken, and which he will in the future speak to us. It is expected that we hearken to the revelations of his will, and adhere to them, cleave to them with all our might; for this is salvation, and any thing short of this clips the salvation and the glory of the Saints. (*Discourses of Brigham Young*, 1998, 220)

This advice is especially meaningful in regard to your patriarchal blessing, for this blessing is direct revelation of the Lord's will on your behalf. How important it is, therefore, to strive every day to live up to the Lord's expectations and work diligently toward the fulfillment of your blessing.

*Some Examples*

Think of a new member of the Church, converted through the faith and diligence of the missionaries in the mission field, who not long thereafter receives his patriarchal blessing. Let's suppose that this young man notes with great interest the references in his blessing to the joy that comes from living the gospel, with promises that his sincere prayers will be heard and answered and that the glorious harvest of enduring to the end will be his through faithfulness and obedience.

Will he not retain such promised joy in his mind every day of his life? Will he not be edified to know that his Father in Heaven loves him and has prepared these marvelous blessings for him over the years?

Similarly, think of a young woman who learns through her patriarchal blessing that her life will be filled with joy beyond measure as she grows in spiritual maturity and takes on the qualities reflected in the life and mission of Jesus Christ. How will she feel as she encounters the inevitable detours of life where adversity and tribulation can all too easily sow the seeds of sorrow and discontent? Will her patriarchal blessing not provide comfort in giving her hope of an overarching joy that will eventually transcend life's sorrows and give her peace and serenity through the gospel of Christ? As this young woman studies the scriptures, will she not find assurance in passages like this one from the apostle Paul (recalling the words of Isaiah): "But as it is written, Eye hath not seen, nor ear heard, neither have entered into the heart of man, the things which God hath prepared for them that love him. But God hath revealed them unto us by his Spirit: for the Spirit searcheth all things, yea, the deep things of God" (1 Corinth. 2:9–10)? Thus we can see that a patriarchal blessing provides the framework for attaining enduring happiness and joy—the fruits of the gospel of Christ through the Atonement.

Finally, consider the example of a young man who is promised in his patriarchal blessing that he will come forth on the morning of the first resurrection to take his place among the elect of Zion. Such a thought will expand his perspective as he ponders the glories of a future life in the mansions of the Father and the Son, where the faithful are clothed with immortality and eternal life. Where in all of the world can this kind of vista of everlasting joy be planted in the hearts of God's children with as much enduring power as through personal revelation that comes in a patriarchal blessing? Will this young man not remember, day by day, his grand potential to become one of the elect of Zion? Will he not be more watchful to keep himself clean and obedient to all the commandments, remembering his covenants faithfully? Such is the power of a patriarchal blessing given by inspiration through the Spirit of Truth.

*Ideas for Finding Joy in the Fulfillment of Your Patriarchal Blessing*

Here are several ideas for you to think about and follow in your daily life as you strive to become a better follower of the Savior:

- Realize that obedience is a reflection of your faith and love. With increased faith in and abundant love for God, you will choose to obey by following the counsel in your patriarchal blessing. If you align yourself with lasting values and principles, obedience will be an exciting journey, not something viewed as a restriction on your behavior.

- Understand that the Lord wants you to be free. Look at obedience as a doorway to more freedom rather than a straitjacket on your lifestyle. The Lord's laws and rules are made to enhance freedom to the highest degree for the greatest number of people.

- Be prepared to accept consequences. All laws have consequences. An example would be the laws of health and well-being. Obedience to such laws is purely and simply in your best interest. The rewards are built in. It is wise to gain knowledge concerning the benefits of obedience to the law. The upholding of God's laws brings the blessings of safety, peace, and security to your family and to society. As you fulfill the essence of your patriarchal blessing, you will enjoy great blessings of peace and happiness. Failing to live up to the promises in your patriarchal blessing may well result in the loss of the divine blessings that the Lord has in store. It is your choice.

- Be an example in your family and community. Teach others obedience through your example and love rather than through the exercise of power and control. Help others understand and appreciate the reasons why we should keep the Lord's commandments. Make it a quest in your life to live up to every aspect of your patriarchal blessing, both for yourself as well as for your family. Such success raises self-confidence and the ability to gain self-discipline, which has its own rewards. Overcome fear through your love of God and your desire to obey His commandments.

# FREQUENTLY ASKED QUESTIONS

*Can I still have a father's blessing?*

The father is the natural patriarch in the family. He has a right to give a father's blessing to his children and can even give a patriarchal blessing to them. A blessing of this type is not recorded to be stored in the Church archives, but it can be recorded for the family or for the individual. You should seek blessings from your father or grandfather (or any priesthood bearer who might have stewardship over you) so that you might receive blessings from your Heavenly Father to carry out your duties and responsibilities or for comfort or well-being. The purpose of the priesthood is to bless lives, and a father's blessing or a priesthood blessing is meant for just that purpose: to bless the lives of Heavenly Father's children. In this case, that means you personally.

*Why is it important to reread my patriarchal blessing often?*

As you mature in life and have different roles and stewardships placed upon you, you will see things with different perspectives and changing perceptions. Therefore, it is important to read and reread your blessing prayerfully from time to time and examine its relevance for all important aspects in your life.

*How can my patriarchal blessing be fulfilled?*

As with all blessings, your patriarchal blessing is conditioned upon your faithfulness and obedience. The Lord has declared, "There is a law, irrevocably decreed in heaven before the foundations of this world, upon which all blessings are predicated—And when we obtain any blessing from God, it is by obedience to that law upon which it is predicated" (D&C 130:20–21). Once you receive your patriarchal blessing, it is important that you do all within your power to fulfill it with faith and devotion. That means humbly receiving and acting on the admonitions given. It also means following the cautions mentioned in order to avoid or transcend the trials and tribulations referred to. In this way, you can enjoy the promised blessings and grow in stature and wisdom as a child of God. To make a patriarchal blessing part of your life, you must live worthy of it. Act as if it were a statement of reality, and it will become such through your faith, your diligence, and the heed that you give it.

*If I have made mistakes, will I ever be able to repent and reclaim the blessings I was promised when I received my blessing?*

In regard to reclaiming blessings pronounced upon one's head, either as a priesthood blessing or a patriarchal blessing, James E. Faust has said, "I humbly and prayerfully urge any who for any reason may not have lived so as to realize a fulfillment of the priesthood blessings pronounced upon them to so order their lives as to reclaim those blessings" ("Priesthood Blessings," *Ensign,* Nov. 1995, 62).

# THE GIFT OF A
## PATRIARCHAL BLESSING

Remember that Heavenly Father and His Son Jesus Christ love you. Your family and Church leaders love you and hope the very best for you as you grow and prosper in the kingdom of God. Your patriarchal blessing is very special, for it is the voice of the Lord speaking to you from the heavens through the Holy Ghost. Your patriarchal blessing is personal revelation to guide you day by day, year by year, as you navigate the pathways of life and prepare to take your place as a son or daughter of God in the mansions of the Father, crowned with glory and eternal life.

ED PINEGAR is a retired dentist and long-time teacher of early-morning seminary and religion classes at Brigham Young University. He teaches at the Joseph Smith Academy and has served as a mission president in England and at the Missionary Training Center in Provo, Utah. He has been a bishop twice and a stake president and is a temple sealer. Ed and his wife, Patricia, have eight children, thirty-five grandchildren, and five great-grandchildren and reside in Orem, Utah.

RICHARD ALLEN is a husband, father, teacher, and writer. He has served on several high councils, in several stake presidencies, and as a bishop. Richard's teaching assignments in the Church have included service as a full-time missionary, instructor in various priesthood quorums, gospel doctrine teacher, and stake institute instructor. He has served as a faculty member at Brigham Young University and The Johns Hopkins University. Richard has authored or coauthored many articles, manuals, and books and has served on a number of national educational boards. He and his wife, Carol Lynn Hansen Allen, have four children and five grandchildren.